ECDL

for Microsoft Office 2

Basic Concepts of
Information Technology

ECDL3

module 1

for Microsoft Office 2000

Brendan Munnelly and Paul Holden

Basic Concepts of Information Technology

Everything you need to pass the European Computer Driving Licence®, module by module

An imprint of **Pearson Education**

London · New York · Sydney · Tokyo · Singapore · Madrid · Mexico City · Munich · Paris

PEARSON EDUCATION LIMITED

Head Office:
Edinburgh Gate
Harlow CM20 2JE
Tel: +44 (0)1279 623623
Fax: +44 (0)1279 431059

London Office:
128 Long Acre
London WC2E 9AN
Tel: +44 (0)20 7447 2000
Fax: +44 (0)20 7240 5771

Website: www.it-minds.com

This edition published in Great Britain in 2002
First published as part of *ECDL3 The Complete Coursebook for Microsoft Office 2000* in 2002

© Rédacteurs Software Documentation Limited 2002

ISBN 0-130-35458-9

British Library Cataloguing in Publication Data
A CIP catalogue record for this book can be obtained from the British Library

Rédacteurs Limited is at http://www.redact.ie

Brendan Munnelly is at http://www.munnelly.com

10 9 8 7 6 5 4 3 2 1

Typeset by Pantek Arts Ltd, Maidstone, Kent.
Printed and bound in Great Britain by Ashford Colour Press, Gosport, Hampshire.

The Publishers' policy is to use paper manufactured from sustainable forests.

Preface

The European Computer Driving Licence (ECDL) is an internationally recognized qualification in end-user computer skills. It is designed to give employers and job-seekers a standard against which they can measure competence – not in theory, but in practice. Its seven Modules cover the areas most frequently required in today's business environment. More than one million people in over fifty countries have undertaken ECDL in order to benefit from the personal, social and business advantages, and international mobility that it provides.

In addition to its application in business, the ECDL has a social and cultural purpose. With the proliferation of computers into every aspect of modern life, there is a danger that society will break down into two groups – the information 'haves' and the information 'have nots'. The seven modules of the ECDL are not difficult, but they equip anyone who passes them to participate actively and fully in the Information Society.

The ECDL is not product-specific – you can use any hardware or software to perform the tasks in the examinations. And you can take the seven examinations in any order, and work through the syllabus at your own pace.

This book is one of a set of seven, each dealing with one of the ECDL modules.

Welcome to the world of computers!

CONTENTS

Introduction

Learning about computers for the first time is rather like learning about a foreign country. A land where words like 'megabyte' and 'peripheral' are part of the everyday conversation. The only crop grown and harvested is something called 'data'. And it is important not only to be faster than your neighbour, but smaller too!

But you need to learn about this country. It was once an out-of-the-way place that attracted only handfuls of scientists to its shores. Now no other destination is more popular.

Like all good tourist guides, this module introduces you gently to the more commonly spoken words of the computer dialect. It points out the major landmarks (the hard disk, memory, and processor are all places you need to take in). And it steers you away from the pitfalls that most offend native computer speakers – such as confusing an 'operating system' with an 'application program'.

Have a pleasant trip. And good luck!

CHAPTER 1

A short history of computing

In this chapter

This chapter gives you a brief overview of the history of commercial computing, and paints a picture of the role of computers in the world today.

New skills

At the end of this chapter, you should know that computers:

- Have been developed relatively recently
- Become faster, more reliable, and cheaper every year
- Are being used widely in business and education

A long line of machines

From earliest times, people have counted things, measured things, kept records of things, and told other people about things. The 'things' could have been the number of sheep in a flock, the weight of a child, the size of a field, the length of time since the last drought, or the intensity of an earthquake.

From earliest times, people used tools and techniques to help them count more reliably, measure more accurately, record more indelibly, transmit more clearly – they used, for example, measuring tapes, slide rules, sextants, weighing scales, and clocks.

The computer is simply the latest in this long line of calculating and recording machines. That's all it is. Everything we see computers doing today – and we see them doing a lot – they are doing because they can calculate and they can store the results of their calculations.

However, this principle is masked by one outstanding fact: what computers do may be simple, but they do an incredible amount of work, quickly and reliably. The speed of computers today is measured in millions of operations per second. The operations may be simple, but they can be combined in all sorts of ways to yield a vast array of useful functions.

This has almost all come about within the last thirty or forty years, which is the entire length of the history of commercial computers.

In the 1960s, a commercial computer occupied a large air-conditioned room; needed a team of specialists to operate it; consumed vast amounts of electricity; and frequently broke down.

Today's computers are typically much smaller and faster: what previously took up a full room fits into a small box. They can store more information; they consume less power; and they have become far easier to operate.

To give you some idea of the speed of advance, the first personal computers (PCs) were launched in 1979, with a clock speed (don't worry about it – it's just how we measure the speed of computers) of about 5 megahertz (MHz). Today, if you go out to buy a new PC, it is unlikely that you will be offered anything less than 400 MHz or even 500 MHz – eighty or one hundred times as fast. Similar progress has been made in the other main measure of computer power – storage capacity.

You don't need to understand how this has been achieved, and you don't need to know all the details. However, you should be aware of the speed of progress and the main ways in which it is measured. So, if you go out to buy a computer, you will at least know what questions to ask, and will understand the answers.

Every year, computers are becoming smaller, faster, cheaper, more reliable, and easier to use. They are being used in all sorts of situations where it would previously have been impossible to use them: not only in business and government, but also in education, entertainment, health care, sport, art, and design. You see computers in homes, clubs, and restaurants; you don't see them (but they are there) in car engines, bank automatic teller machines, supermarket checkouts, washing machines, telephone systems, and video recorders. You are probably wearing one at this moment, on your wrist, buried inside your watch.

System unit

Screen

(Monitor, VDU)

Loudspeakers

Mouse

Keyboard

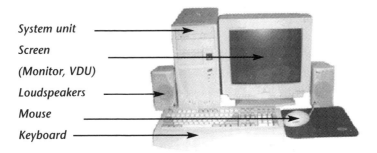

You're surrounded.

But you're *not* under threat: computers are machines, tools. They are designed by people to meet people's needs; they are operated by people. People turn them on. People turn them off.

People like you.

The ECDL is designed to take the fear out of computing, to give you the knowledge and the skills you need to use this technology. With this book, you will learn about the most common PC applications. You won't learn everything: it is not necessary to know everything – it's not even possible. What this book aims to do is to teach you *enough* – enough to perform most of the tasks that most people do most of the time, and to give you enough confidence to tackle the unknown, and to learn from experience.

Self test 1: History of computing

1 Today's PCs are approximately how much faster than the first PCs?

   a ❏   Five times as fast

   b ❏   Ten times as fast

   c ❏   A hundred times as fast

   d ❏   A thousand times as fast

2 Which of the following devices may incorporate a computer? (Pick as many as you think do, and, for each, say what the computer might do.)

   a ❏   A car engine

   b ❏   A video recorder

   c ❏   A bank cash machine

   d ❏   A bicycle

3 **True or false**: In the 1960s, computers were built by hand from stronger materials. As a result, they were more reliable than today's computers, which are mass-produced, smaller, and more delicate.

4 **True or false**: Because of the tiny size of modern computers, they are very hard to make, virtually impossible to repair, and as a result, very expensive.

Chapter summary: so now you know

The computer is the latest in a long line of tools used to perform calculations and store the results. As they have developed, they have become faster, more reliable, and capable of storing more information. These developments have enabled them to be applied in many areas of commercial life, administration, education, and entertainment.

CHAPTER 2

What exactly is a computer?

In this chapter

In this chapter you will learn what distinguishes a computer from other machines. You will also learn about the different types of computer in use today.

New skills

At the end of this chapter you should know:
- What a computer is
- The difference between hardware and software
- The various categories of computers

New words

At the end of this chapter you should be able to explain the following terms:
- Hardware
- Software
- PC
- Mainframe
- Dumb terminal
- Intelligent terminal

The trouble with definitions

I t is relatively easy to define a washing machine, motor car, or telephone: these devices may be complicated and technologically advanced, but we can talk about them in terms of what they do. They wash clothes, transport people from A to B, and enable people to hold conversations with one another over a distance.

As we saw in the previous section, a computer can be used for almost anything – including controlling the different washing cycles in a washing machine.

In fact, the first part of our definition of a computer recognises this fact: computers are *general-purpose* machines. The same computer can operate over a few hours as a typewriter, desktop publishing studio, sound editor, video editor, accounts tracker, e-mail sender, an internet browser, etc.

When you flick the light switch, the light comes on: you could say that the light has obeyed your instruction. Well, computers respond in the same way to instructions: these instructions are called *programs*. And programs are written to make computers behave in specific ways: to act as word processors or to control generating stations. Computers are *programmable*.

Different programs enable the same computer to operate under different guises. We could leave our definition at that, but it will help to add two other ideas: computers can *calculate*, and they can *store* the results of their calculations.

Computer

A computer is a general-purpose, programmable device that is capable of calculating and storing results.

One way of thinking about a computer is as a 'black box' that accepts input on one side, processes it in some way, and then produces output on the other side.

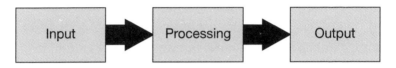

The input might be a mathematical problem, the supplier invoices for the month, a search for a good restaurant in Sydney, or the temperature of a furnace. The output might be the answer to the mathematical problem, the cheques to pay the invoices, the name and address of the restaurant, or the instructions to shut the control valves on the fuel supply.

What goes on inside the black box is called *processing*: the manipulation of the input necessary to produce the output.

However, the black box is not magic: everything – *everything* – going into a computer is first converted into numbers, and all forms of output – including text on the page, graphics on the screen, music, even telephone conversations – have to be converted into their final form from numbers. In the middle – inside the black box – the numbers are added together in various ways and combinations, under a set of rules called a program. The only magic is the fact that these calculations take place at a rate of millions per second – and, of course, the human ingenuity in the design and the programming.

Computer systems consist of two very different types of elements: *hardware and software.*

- Hardware includes all the physical things that you can touch, feel, weigh, and, on rare occasions, kick.

- Software is the intangible information component – the instructions, or programs that tell the hardware how to behave.

Hardware

Hardware is the term used to describe the physical parts of a computer system.

Software

Software is the term used to describe the instructions that cause the computer system to behave in a given way.

Types of computer

Computers fall into a number of different categories, although the dividing line between the categories is not always clear. At one end of the spectrum are *mainframes*. These are big, expensive machines, typically used by large corporations, governmental organizations, and scientific research establishments. They are expected to run continuously, 24 hours a day, 365 days a year. They are capable of processing huge numbers of transactions, and performing extremely complex calculations.

At the other end of the spectrum are the computers most of us are familiar with – the PC (*personal computer*), formerly known as the *microcomputer*. Today, PCs can be bought for less than £1,000. PCs come in various shapes and sizes. *Desktop* computers are the most common: they generally include a system unit, a screen, and a keyboard, as separate components. *Laptop or notebook* computers are more portable: the screen is a flat *liquid crystal display* (LCD), which forms a lid hinged to cover the keyboard and system unit. Laptops are somewhat more expensive than desktop PCs.

In between these two ends of the computer spectrum lie *minicomputers*, which are typically used by medium-sized enterprises, or by departments within larger organizations. Like mainframes, they offer greater processing power, storage capacity and reliability than PCs.

Network computers (*network servers*) are computers that administer, support, and protect the security of a computer network. Users on a network are able to use the resources (data, software, hardware) on the network server. In the past, such users mainly used *dumb terminals* – devices that simply accepted input from the user and displayed results. All the processing and storage was done by the server. Nowadays, most users have *intelligent terminals* – PCs that have their own 'local' processing and storage capacity.

Self test 2: A computer is...?

1 Distinguish between a computer and a pocket calculator.

    a   ❑   Because the calculator is purpose-built, it is more accurate.

    b   ❑   There is no difference: the calculator contains a computer.

c ❑ The computer includes a word-processor; the calculator doesn't.

d ❑ The computer has a bigger screen.

2 Which of the following statements is/are true?

a ❑ Cables and other flexible parts of a computer are called software; all the solid parts are called hardware.

b ❑ Hardware is the term used to describe the physical parts of a computer system.

c ❑ Diskettes and CDs are software; the screen and keyboard are hardware.

d ❑ Software is another word for programs.

3 Which of the following statements is/are true?

a ❑ A mainframe is a large computer built in the 1960s or 1970s that is now obsolete.

b ❑ A mainframe is a large computer typically used by a big company or governmental organization.

c ❑ A mainframe is a metal framework inside the plastic casing of a computer.

d ❑ A mainframe is another word for hardware.

4 A microcomputer is often called a PC. The abbreviation PC stands for:

a ❑ Personal computer

b ❑ Portable computer

c ❑ Politically correct

d ❑ Personal calculator

e ❑ Professional capacity

5   Which of the following is/are portable computer(s)?

   a   ❑   Minicomputer

   b   ❑   Microcomputer

   c   ❑   Laptop

   d   ❑   Notebook

6   Which of the following statements is/are true?

   a   ❑   A network server is another name for a dumb terminal.

   b   ❑   A dumb terminal is useless without a network server.

   c   ❑   A network server is useless without a dumb terminal.

   d   ❑   A dumb terminal is a computer without any loudspeakers.

   e   ❑   An intelligent terminal is a computer used for military or industrial espionage.

   f   ❑   An intelligent terminal is another name for a bank cash machine.

Chapter summary: so now you know

Computers are general-purpose machines. What distinguishes a computer calculating a payroll from one forecasting the weather is the program it is running. And in fact the *same* computer could be programmed to do both tasks.

Computers accept information from the outside (input), do something to it (processing), and display or print out the results (output). The two main elements in a computer system are *hardware*, which is the term used for the physical parts, and *software*, which describes the instructions or programs that cause the computer to behave in a given way.

The most familiar computers are called PCs or microcomputers. The biggest and most expensive – used by large organizations – are called mainframes. In between are minicomputers.

A computer network is controlled by a network computer, or network server. The devices connected to the server are called terminals. These may be dumb terminals – with no processing or storage power of their own – or intelligent terminals – with their own processing and storage capability.

CHAPTER 3

Computer hardware

In this chapter

When you go out to buy a computer, you are immediately faced with a range of options that even experienced computer people find bewildering. To make a sensible choice, you need to know the function of the main components in a computer system, and the criteria upon which you should base your decision.

A typical PC system is made up of a number of components. Some of these are essential, and some optional. In some cases, a number of alternatives are available, from which you have to choose.

This chapter takes you on a tour of the typical computer system, and identifies all the hardware components. We look first at the components that are normally inside the main *system unit* ('in the box'), and then at the other components in a typical system ('outside the box').

New skills

At the end of this section, you should be able to:
- Name the hardware components in a computer system
- Say what each component is for
- Describe some of the 'optional extras'
- Describe how to look after your computer

New words

At the end of this section, you should be able to explain the following terms:
- Processor
- Hard disk
- Keyboard
- Mouse
- Modem
- Memory
- Diskette
- Screen
- Printer
- Multimedia

In the box

The system unit – usually a beige or grey box – is the most essential part of the computer. It houses the processor (the 'brain'), the various kinds of memory (described below), and the electronics to control all the other components. It also usually includes a fan, designed to keep the whole unit cool. The fan is responsible for the hum from the computer when you turn it on. The system unit may stand vertically on the floor (a *tower*), or horizontally on the desk, usually with the screen on top (a *desktop* unit). In a *laptop or notebook* computer, the system unit is usually built underneath the keyboard.

Processor

The length of time it takes a computer to perform a task depends on a number of factors. The first of these is the speed of the processor – the chip at the heart of the computer. This is measured in megahertz (MHz), and the bigger the number, the faster the processor (the more calculations it can perform per second). This measure of the computer's performance is so critical that it is usually included in the name of the computer.

The processor chip and the electronics that support it are referred to as the *central processing unit* (CPU).

Processor

The central processing unit (CPU) is the brains of a computer. It is in the CPU that most calculations take place, and the CPU speed largely determines the speed of the computer.

Memory

The definition of a computer includes the idea of storage: the computer has to be able to store the results of its calculations. In practice, a computer has to store a huge amount of information. It has a number of different kinds of memory, two of which are regularly cited in the advertisements for computers: RAM and disk space.

Random Access Memory (RAM)

Random Access Memory (RAM) is used by the computer as a sort of working area while it is carrying out a given task. (It is often called working storage.) Here it holds the list of instructions that it is currently working on, the data on which it is working, and the interim results of its calculations. The 'R' in RAM is its main advantage. It can be accessed randomly, which means that the computer can get at any piece of data directly – it does not have to look through the storage area from the start until it finds the piece of interest. This makes it fast. In general, the more RAM the better, and a certain minimum is required for many programs. RAM is often called *main memory*.

Memory capacity is measured in *bytes*. One byte consists of eight *bits*. You can think of a bit in electrical terms as a switch: on or off, or in mathematical terms as a single binary number: 0 or 1. Eight of these – a byte – can represent a letter of the alphabet, or a single number. You are likely to be offered a new computer with at least 64 megabytes (64 MB – 64 million bytes) or possibly 128 MB of RAM. (This is twice as much as you would have been offered for the same price last year, and probably half as much as you will be offered this time next year.)

Random Access Memory (RAM)

> *RAM is the computer's working memory, and an important factor in determining a computer's speed. RAM is volatile. As soon as power is turned off, whatever data was in RAM is lost.*

It is relatively easy to upgrade the memory on your computer by buying additional memory chips. They are inexpensive and easy to install. Depending on what you are using your computer for, additional memory can make a huge difference to its performance. (Don't, however, attempt to install additional memory without expert guidance.)

Read-Only Memory (ROM)

Don't confuse RAM with another kind of memory that you may occasionally hear of: ROM (Read-Only Memory). This is where the computer stores its low-level programs, particularly the instructions necessary to start the computer. ROM differs from RAM in two ways: first, it is not changed after the computer is assembled (you can read it, but not write to it), and second, its contents remain unchanged even when the power is turned off. (RAM is *volatile* – its contents are erased if the power supply is cut off.)

Read-Only Memory (ROM)

Computers typically contain a small amount of ROM that holds small programs for starting up the computer. Unlike RAM, ROM cannot be written to.

Hard disk

After processor speed and the amount of RAM, the next major determinant of computer power is the amount of disk space. A disk is a device for storing information. It is very different from RAM, for a number of reasons:

- First, disks record information magnetically, in much the same way as music tapes or video tapes. They are not volatile: once the information is recorded, it remains on the disk until it is changed or deleted.

- Second, the process of getting information onto a disk or retrieving information from a disk involves mechanical movement. The disk revolves at a constant, high speed, and a read/write head moves in and out just above the surface of the disk. The *read/write head* can change the polarization of tiny magnetic particles on the surface of the disk, and can detect the polarization of particles. Moving parts eventually wear out and as a result, disks are more likely to malfunction than non-moving RAM. The moving parts also introduce delays into the processes of reading and writing, whereas reading from RAM is almost instantaneous.

Like memory capacity, disk capacity is measured in *bytes*. Disk capacity is bigger by several orders of magnitude: a new computer today will typically come with a 12-gigabyte disk (12 GB – 12 billion bytes) rising to 40 gigabytes.

Let's consider this slowly: 12,000,000,000 bytes. The 32 volumes of *Encyclopaedia Brittanica* contain approximately 44,000,000 words, or approximately 220,000,000 characters (bytes). A 12-GB disk could hold that text almost fifty-six times, yet it only weighs about 1 kilogram, and takes up less space than one of the encyclopaedia's volumes. The amount of information that a disk can hold is the third performance measure that you should consider when buying a computer.

Hard disk

A spinning magnetic disk on which computer data can be stored. Typical storage capacities range from a few to a few tens of gigabytes.

Diskettes, CD-ROMs, DVDs, Zip disks, tapes

The disks described on the previous page are built in to the computer. They are often called *hard disks*. They remain in the computer, and are not (generally) transferred between computers. There is, however, a wide range of removable storage devices that can be transferred easily from one computer to another, or used as security backups in case of loss, damage, or theft of the computer.

Diskettes (floppy disks)

Another kind of disk is the so-called *'floppy disk'* or diskette. (Early removable disks were housed in flexible envelopes, which earned them the name 'floppy'. The more recent design, with which you are probably familiar, uses a hard plastic shell with a sliding metal cover.)

The most common type of diskette holds 1.4 MB. This is enough to hold many typical word-processing documents, so that they can easily be passed from one person to another. You can use a diskette to transfer a document from your office computer to your home computer – simply copy the document to the diskette, and bring it home in your pocket. The entire text of this book (but not the graphics) fits onto a single diskette, with room to spare!

Just as RAM is often referred to as 'working storage' or 'main memory', disks and diskettes are often called 'backing storage', or 'secondary storage'.

Floppy diskette

A small magnetic disk that can be removed from the computer. A diskette typically holds 1.4 MB of information.

CD-ROMs and DVDs

Until quite recently, diskettes were also the principal way of loading programs onto a computer. Nowadays, however, software is most often supplied on CD-ROM (Compact Disk Read-Only Memory). Physically, a CD-ROM is indistinguishable from a music CD, and in fact CD readers in computers are almost all capable of playing music CDs.

The move from diskette to CD-ROM as the favoured medium for distributing software has taken place mainly because of the size of modern software systems: they need more storage space. (More space is required because the programs have added functionality, because they are more graphic in design, and because they may include other multimedia elements.) A single CD-ROM can hold as much information as 460 diskettes – about 650 MB.

CD-ROM drives (the part of the computer that reads CD-ROMs) are now offered as standard on all new computers. The only performance measure to watch out for is the speed of the drive, always quoted as a multiple of the normal music CD-player speed: nowadays, 36× speed or 40× speed CD-ROM drives are normal.

A limitation of standard CD-ROMs is that, while they can be read as often as necessary, they can be written to only once. A newer type of CD-ROM is the CD-ReWritable disk, or CD-RW. You can work with CD-RW drives and disks just as you would with floppy diskettes or hard disks by writing data to them more than once.

CD-ROM

A disk that typically stores about 650 MB of data. Standard CD-ROMs can be written to only once. CD-RW disks can be written to more than once.

CD-ROMs are now being overtaken by DVDs (Digital Versatile Disks), which look similar, but have a great deal more storage capacity – up to 3.9 gigabytes or GB.

To record information on a CD, you need a CD Writer (or 'burner'). Information is encoded on the surface of CDs as tiny holes, which are detected by a laser beam.

Magnetic tape

Magnetic tape – usually in cassettes not unlike music cassettes – is used for distributing software and for keeping backup copies of large volumes of data. It is less useful in normal everyday use, because it cannot be  accessed randomly: the computer has to read it through from the beginning to find the part of interest.

Zip disks, etc.

High-capacity removable diskettes are gaining favour for keeping backups and for transferring large files between computers. Some use magnetic technology, some laser technology. Among the most popular such devices is

the *Zip drive*, which attaches to any computer's parallel port
(printer connection) and provides storage on 100-MB or 250-
MB removable disks.

Medium	Typical capacity	Typical cost of medium (July 2001)
Hard disk (fixed)	12 to 40 gigabytes,	£50 to £300
Diskette	1.4 megabytes	Less than £1
CD	650 megabytes	Less than £10
DVD	5.2 gigabytes	£20 to £30
Zip	250 megabytes	Less than £10
Tape	4 to 100 gigabytes	£20 to £70

Out of the box: the essentials

Everything outside the grey box is peripheral, which is why
all the other objects are called *peripherals*. (Here we're
cheating a little: technically, all secondary storage, such as
disks, CD-ROMs, etc., can be considered to be peripheral as
well.) In most computer systems, the three *essential*
peripherals are the keyboard and mouse (used for input), and
the screen (used for output).

Keyboard

A keyboard is a set of typewriter-like keys that enables you,
the user, to enter information and instructions into a
computer. Keys on a computer keyboard are of three types:

- **Alphanumeric Keys:** Letters and numbers

- **Punctuation Keys:** Comma, full stop, semicolon, and so on

- **Special Keys:** Function keys, control keys, arrow keys, Caps Lock key, and so on.

Screen

The screen looks somewhat like a television. It is also called the monitor (because you use it to monitor what is going on in the computer) or the *visual display unit* (VDU). Most programs are designed in such a way that you appear to enter input directly from the keyboard onto the screen. In fact, you enter it into the processor, and the processor shows you what it has received by displaying it on the screen. Most programs also give you continuous feedback on their progress, and display their output on the screen.

Mouse

Many programs present themselves on the screen as *graphical user interfaces* (GUI – pronounced, believe it or not, 'gooey'). A GUI represents programs, files, and functions as pictures on the screen. The GUI includes a pointer that you can move around the screen until it is at the picture that represents what you want to do. You then indicate your intention, and the program responds accordingly.

The mouse is the tool that you use to move the pointer around the screen. The underside of the mouse houses a ball, and, as you move the mouse over your desk, this ball detects the movements, and converts them into movements of the pointer. Move the mouse left, the pointer moves left; right, and the pointer moves right; push the mouse away from you, and the pointer moves up the screen; pull it towards you, the pointer moves down. After a very short time moving the pointer becomes second nature.

Note that the ball only moves (and therefore the pointer only moves) when the underside of the mouse is in contact with the desk. So you can move the pointer a long distance in one direction by making a series of short moves in that direction with the mouse, each time lifting the mouse so that the return journey does not affect the position of the pointer.

The mouse has two or three buttons on top: these are used to signal to the computer that the pointer has arrived where you want to go. You press one or other buttons once (called a *click*), or twice in quick succession (called a *double-click*).

The mouse (or whatever pointing device you use – see *Other pointing devices* on the next page) makes operation of the computer easy, and even intuitive, but it is seldom absolutely necessary. Most programs allow you to move the pointer around the screen and choose your options using special keys or combinations of keys on the keyboard. Some users prefer this: it means they can do all their work from the keyboard – they don't have to switch back and forth between the keyboard and the mouse.

Other pointing devices

Mice are by far the most common pointing devices, but there
are others.

- **Trackballs**: These are like upside-down mice: you move
  the pointer by manipulating a ball in a special housing
  with your fingers. Trackballs are useful in situations
  where desk space is limited.

- **Joysticks and games controllers**: These fulfil the same
  function as the mouse or trackball, but are designed
  specially for games and simulation.

- **Touchpads**: Most portable computers have a device built
  in to the keyboard for moving the pointer, either in the
  form of a miniature joystick, or a pressure-sensitive
  touchpad that detects movements of your finger.

- **Light pens**: These are pen-shaped devices that, when
  placed close to the screen, can be used both to draw
  and to control icons or choices shown on the screen.

- **Touch screens**: You will often see these seen in public
  information kiosks: the user simply touches the screen
  at the point of interest in order to exercise a choice
  from the options displayed.

- **Graphics tablets**: These are flat surfaces that detect the
  movement of a plastic stylus (pen) across them. They
  are typically used for art and design applications, but
  smaller versions are becoming common in 'pocket',
  'hand-held' or 'palmtop' computers. These devices
  (known as *personal digital assistants*, or PDAs) are too
  small to allow typing.

Out of the box: optional extras

Without the components described in the previous section, it would be hard to get the computer to do anything useful. There are a number of other devices that, although they are not essential, are normal parts of the system in the home, school or office. These are a printer, a modem, and loudspeakers. Some others – scanners, digital cameras, microphones – would have been considered exotic a couple of years ago, but are increasingly considered 'normal'.

Printers

There are several kinds of printer on the market: the two most common are:

- **Laser printers**: These use a technology similar to that used in photocopying to transfer the image of a page onto paper. The image is 'drawn' under instruction from the computer.

- **Inkjet printers**: These have a moving 'pen' (the *write head*) that holds an ink cartridge. This moves back and forth over the page and, under computer control, ejects a minute quantity of ink at the precise point where it is required on the page.

You will occasionally come across a third category of printer: *impact printers*. These work like a typewriter: they hammer out the required characters onto the page through an ink-impregnated (or carbon-covered) ribbon. There are several kinds, using slightly different techniques for making the marks on the paper: dot matrix printers, daisy wheel printers, and line printers. Nowadays their use is confined to specialist applications (printing receipts from cash registers, printing the time of arrival on a ticket in a car park), or high-volume printouts that do not use graphics (tax forms, electricity bills).

Plotters are used in specialist applications, such as producing architectural or engineering drawings. Most of them are designed to produce large drawings accurately. They are relatively expensive.

How to choose a printer

Some of the factors you should consider when buying a printer are:

- **Speed of output**: Most laser printers can print 8 or 12 pages a minute. This speed may depend on what you are printing: graphics, or text pages with a variety of different fonts, tend to be slower. If you need a faster printer, be prepared to pay a lot more.

  Inkjet printers are generally a lot slower than laser printers, but their speed doesn't depend on what you are printing. The quality of the print tends to vary, because they rely on a moving write head.

- **Colour**: If you want colour output, you have to buy a colour printer. It's that simple. Colour laser printers are expensive; colour inkjet printers are only slightly more expensive than black-and-white printers.

Some colour printers use three different inks to produce their output, some four. Some use a combined three- or four-colour cartridge, some a separate cartridge for each colour. Your choice depends on what you are using the printer for. If you are only occasionally using colour output, make sure you have a separate black cartridge: the density of the black printout from a black cartridge is much higher than that from a combination of colours. If you get a combined four-colour cartridge, you will be throwing out the almost-full colour inks just because you have run out of black.

- **Cost of consumables**: The initial cost of the printer is only one of the cost factors that you need to consider: ink cartridges (for inkjet printers) and toner cartridges (for laser printers) have to be replaced regularly, and it is worthwhile calculating the cost per page of output before making your final decision.

Modem

A *modem* is used to connect your computer to the telephone network, so that you can send e-mail, or use the internet. Most computers sold today include a modem already installed in the system unit, but they can also be obtained as external devices that are connected to the computer by a cable. Most modems can enable your computer to function as a fax machine (although, unless you have a scanner, you are limited to sending text-only faxes).

Multimedia

Computers can manipulate any kind of data that can be converted into numbers, including music, pictures, animated drawings, video, and speech. A range of applications has grown up around this capability, in which text, video, and sound are mixed to deliver instruction, information, or entertainment. These applications are called *multimedia applications*, and a computer that can run them is often called a *multimedia computer*. Most computers nowadays can run these applications. However, if this is your main interest, you may want to consider a computer with a larger screen, and more advanced sound generation and video display capabilities. In addition, a number of specialized peripherals are available.

Scanner

Think of a scanner as the first half of a photocopier – it copies a photograph, drawing, or page of text into the computer, where you can use a program to manipulate it, or print it out (like the second half of the photocopier). You can use the scanner to include a drawing or photograph in a newsletter, or use *optical character recognition* (OCR) software to decipher the text, and use all or part of it in a word-processing document (without having to re-type it).

Digital camera

A digital camera works exactly like a standard camera, except that it does not use photographic film – the images are recorded digitally in the camera's memory. From there, you can transfer them to your computer and subsequently print them out, use graphics software to edit them, archive them for posterity, or e-mail them to your friends.

Loudspeakers

Loudspeakers are standard equipment on almost all new computers. They are used to play music and other sounds.

Sound Cards

Again, your system unit almost certainly includes a sound card, which is used to control all the audio output (music, speech, etc.). However, if the quality of music output is important to you, you may want to upgrade from the sound card supplied as standard equipment.

Microphone

Many software applications can be controlled by speech commands. These are spoken into a microphone.

Multimedia

The use of computers to present text, graphics, video animation and sound in an integrated manner. Hardware elements include scanners, sound cards, loudspeakers, and microphones.

Looking after your hardware

Modern computers are robust and reliable: once they start working, they tend to go on working. But remember that they are sensitive instruments, and avoid testing their tolerance.

DO give your computer room to breathe: it has to have access to fresh air so that the fan can keep the electronics cool.

DON'T block the air vents by stacking books or magazines or (worse) draping clothes over the back of the computer.

DO keep the computer dry. Excessive moisture can play havoc with electric circuitry.

DON'T eat or drink while using your computer: crumbs can clog up your keyboard. A spilt cup of coffee can wreck your computer and (probably worse) cause the loss of all your files stored on the computer.

DO keep your computer free of dust: you will notice that it tends to attract dust. Clean the air vents occasionally, and use an anti-static wipe on the screen.

DON'T expose your computer to extremes of temperature.

DO shut down the computer in an orderly fashion, by systematically closing the applications you have opened.

DON'T just switch it off or pull the plug from the socket.

DO keep diskettes away from the screen: the strong magnetic field generated by the screen may erase or change some of the data.

DON'T move the system unit while the computer is in operation – you risk damaging the hard disk drive.

When something goes wrong

You are more likely to be a computer user than a computer engineer. Therefore respect your PC as a delicate instrument – if it seems to be malfunctioning, don't try to fix it. You risk destroying it or electrocuting yourself. Always call a person qualified to deal with the problem.

Self test 3: Hardware

1 Which of the following is/are essential pieces of
   hardware for a computer to work?

   a ❑ Processor

   b ❑ Scanner

   c ❑ Hammer

   d ❑ Word processor

2 The C in CPU stands for:

   a ❑ Central

   b ❑ Computer

   c ❑ Complex

   d ❑ Computing

   e ❑ Commercial

3 What is a scanner used for?

4 What is a modem used for?

5 The speed of a computer is measured in:

   a ❑ CPUs

   b ❑ MHz

   c ❑ MB

   d ❑ K

   e ❑ RAM

   f ❑ GUIs

6 The R in ROM stands for:

   a ❏   Random

   b ❏   Read

   c ❏   Regular

   d ❏   Right

7 The R in RAM stands for:

   a ❏   Random

   b ❏   Read

   c ❏   Regular

   d ❏   Right

8 Correct any of the following statements that are wrong.

   a ❏   There are exactly eight bytes in a bit.

   b ❏   A megabyte is double the size of a normal byte.

   c ❏   100K bytes is equal to a GB.

   d ❏   A gigabyte is approximately equal to
          1,000,000,000 bytes.

9 Which of the following statements is/are true?

   a ❏   Information stored in RAM is erased when the
          computer is turned off.

   b ❏   Information stored in ROM is erased when the
          computer is turned off.

   c ❏   The M in RAM stands for memory.

   d ❏   The M in ROM stands for memory.

   e ❏   Hard disks, diskettes, and CD-ROMs are all used
          to store computer programs.

10 Name three kinds of pointing device.

11 Name the two most common types of printer.

12 Which can store more information: a high-density diskette or a Zip disk?

Chapter summary: so now you know

The basic PC consists of a *system unit*, a screen, and a keyboard. Virtually all PCs include a pointing device – most commonly a *mouse*.

Inside the system unit are the *processor* or CPU (the 'brains' of the computer), RAM (working memory), ROM (for holding the computer's start-up instructions), hard disk (for holding large amounts of data), and some removable storage – usually a *diskette* and a CD-ROM drive.

Other items that are almost essential are a *printer* and a *modem*. A modem is used to connect the computer to the telephone network, so that you can send and receive e-mail or access the internet.

Many – even most – PCs sold today are equipped for *multimedia*: they include loudspeakers, sound cards, and microphones.

To capture images, drawings, or photographs and include them in newsletters, project reports, or e-mails, you need a *scanner* or a *digital camera*.

Finally, you learnt how to look after your computer, so that it gives a long life of good service.

CHAPTER 4

Software and data

In this chapter

In this chapter you will learn more about the different kinds of software and how they are made. You will also learn what the most valuable part of a computer system is – the data.

New skills

At the end of this chapter you should be able to:
- Distinguish between system software and application software
- Describe the process of software development
- Discuss software licensing and the different types of licence
- Describe how to protect software and data from unauthorized access, loss or damage, and computer viruses
- State the principles of data copyright
- State the principles of data protection and the main provisions of the European Data Protection Directive

New words

At the end of this chapter you should be able to explain the following terms:

- System software
- Application software
- Graphical user interface
- Licensed software
- Freeware
- Shareware
- Systems analyst
- Programmer
- Backup
- Virus
- Copyright
- Data protection

Software

S oftware is the intangible side of computing: it is the generic name given to all the programs – the sets of instructions – that determine how the computer behaves. We distinguish between two kinds of software: *system software* and *application software*.

- System software is concerned with the computer itself – what devices it can control, how it manages files and storage, and how it deals with exceptional conditions.

- Application software is concerned with the world outside the computer – the world of business, entertainment, or education.

Software

The programs (sets of instructions) that determine how the computer behaves.

System software

The main piece of system software that we are concerned with is the *operating system* (OS). This is the driving program of the PC: without it, the PC would be virtually unusable. All other programs depend on the operating system to communicate with and control the hardware. The operating system also controls the timing of different events to make sure they happen in the correct sequence, and manages access to data to ensure security and integrity.

When you add a new piece of hardware to your system, you might have to load a special piece of software called a *driver* to enable the operating system to control the hardware. Older PCs use an operating system called DOS (Disk Operating System). To use DOS, you have to type in commands such as DIR, COPY, or REN.

System software (operating system)

Software that performs such tasks as recognizing input from the keyboard and mouse, sending output to the screen, communicating with printers and other peripherals, and keeping track of files.

Graphical user interface

More recent computers present their operating system through a *graphical user interface* (GUI). The GUI represents all the computer's resources – the hardware resources such as disks and printers, the software resources, including both system software and application programs, and the data files on which you can work – as small pictures or symbols called *icons*. You use the mouse to move the pointer to the icon representing the object you want to use, and press (or *click*) the mouse button to signal your request. This is considerably easier than having to remember a command and typing it accurately. Examples of GUIs include Windows, MacOS, and SunOS.

Application software

Nobody wants to use a lawnmower, or a telephone, or a satellite: what they want to do is cut the grass, talk to their friends, or predict the weather. Similarly, you don't really want to use a computer: you want to use a computer to do *something else*. That 'something else' is your application, and the program that enables you to do it is called the *application program*. By the time you have finished this book you will be able to use several application programs: word processing, spreadsheets, electronic mail, and so on. Some application programs are very common – it is hard to find an office that doesn't use Microsoft Word or Excel or various internet browsers such as Netscape Navigator or Microsoft Explorer. Many computers are sold with these applications pre-loaded.

Application Software

Programs that do real work for users. For example, word processors, spreadsheets, and database management systems.

Other applications are developed for more specialised tasks. People and organizations purchase them in accordance with their particular needs. An architect might use a sophisticated drawing package to design houses; a submarine builder might purchase a piece of project management software to help keep track of the thousands of components. In Chapter 6 we will look in more detail at the types of applications in daily use in business, administration, education, entertainment, and communication.

How software is made

The development of any software system involves a cycle of research, analysis, development, and testing, involving the following types of people:

- **Systems analysts**: They study the business processes that the software is intended to support, and produce the design for the software. They decide what the software should do (but not necessarily how it should do it). You can think of the systems analyst as the software architect. Systems analysts are focused on the needs of the users and the application area.

- **Programmers**: They translate the design into a working program. They write instructions that tell the computer what to do in order to accomplish the task for which the system is intended. You can think of the programmer as the software builder. Programmers are focused on the computer, its capabilities, and its limitations.

Software copyright

Software generally is *licensed* rather than sold. When you buy a software package, you don't own the software: you gain the right to use it under specified conditions. Most personal computer software licences allow you to run the program on only one machine and to make copies of the software only for backup purposes.

In general, software is easy to duplicate, so it is easy for unscrupulous people to make unauthorized copies: don't do it. It's piracy; it's illegal; and it deprives an individual developer or a company of their rightful income, which they need to produce the next version of that piece of software, or the next application that you will want to use.

Don't accept software from dubious sources, whether in person, by mail-order, or over the internet. You are responsible for the legality of the software that you use.

Licensed software

Software that may be used only when the relevant user organization or individual has purchased the right to do so under certain conditions.

Some software, called *freeware* is distributed without charge: you find it on disks given away with magazines, or download it from the internet. Again, you should be clear about the terms of use: in most cases, you can use it, but you may not, for example, sell it for profit, change it in any way, or label it as if it was your own product.

Freeware

Copyrighted software given away without charge by the author. Typically, the author allows people to use the software, but not sell it.

Other software is called *shareware*. It is widely distributed in much the same way as freeware. You can try it out, but if you decide to use it you are expected to send a licence fee to the developer. In some cases, this is based on honour; in other cases, the shareware version will not function after a time period (typically 30 days), or certain functions are disabled in some way. When you register with the developer and send the licence fee, you are given a fully working copy of the software, or a password to unlock the disabled functions.

Shareware

Software that is typically available free of charge, but the author usually requests that you pay a small fee if you like the program and use it regularly. Registered users can receive service assistance and updates.

Problems with software

Software – even the smallest piece of application software – is complex. It is difficult to test thoroughly, because it is difficult to imagine every possible input in every possible combination. Sometimes mistakes are made, or unusual circumstances are not adequately catered for by the designers or programmers.

When the software produces incorrect or unexpected results, it is said to have a *bug*. Bugs can range from minor irritations, where, for example, the screen displays are inconsistent, through significant errors, such as incorrect totals on invoices, to total collapse.

The Millennium Bug

An example of a problem caused by short-sighted programming practices was the so-called 'Millennium Bug'. Many programs stored dates as six digits – two each for day, month and year. For most purposes, this was fine, but when you use these dates in calculations, difficulties can arise. For example, is someone born on 06 01 99 just over a year old or one hundred years old? Such ambiguities can be of critical importance in calculating interest payments, sell-by dates, eligibility for pensions, and so on. Although this problem may seem trivial, putting it right costs businesses around the world many millions of pounds.

When the computer 'freezes' – it ceases to function, refuses to accept any input, won't produce any output – we say that it *hangs*. When this happens, you may be able to resort to an old trick: press three of the keyboard keys simultaneously – CTRL, ALT, and DEL. Most of the time, this will enable you to shut down the offending program, and continue working on something else. Pressing this key combination *twice* generally causes your computer to restart.

Infrequently, a bug will cause the whole system to *crash*. The only solution is to turn off the power, wait a minute, and then turn it on again. A quicker way to achieve the same end is to press the Reset button on your system unit. Treat this as a last resort, however – you will lose any work done since you last saved in all the applications that you have open at the time.

Data

We haven't yet dealt in any detail with data. Data is another intangible in a computer system, but it is not generally built by the software developer. It's built by users – people like you.

So to write a letter, you need a keyboard, a screen, and a

printer (hardware), and you need a word-processing program (software). The letter itself, and the name and address of the recipient, are *data*.

Data is held on a computer system in *files*. Files are organized into *directories* (otherwise known as *folders*). Files and directories are given *names*, so that you can find them and recognize them when you need them, and so that the operating system can find them and work on them when it needs to.

Looking after your data

In most computer systems, the data is the most important element. Hardware and software are easily replaced if they break down, or are lost or stolen. Data, on the other hand, can represent years of work, and may be irreplaceable. So it makes sense to look after it. Data can be lost, corrupted, damaged, or abused in a variety of ways, accidentally or deliberately.

Security and passwords

You can protect your data against theft, corruption, and prying eyes by using a system of *passwords*. Depending on the application, you can use passwords to decide who can see the data and who can change it.

Most applications allow you to choose your own password, and encourage you to change it frequently. Choose a password that is not too obvious – if it is easy to guess, its purpose may be defeated. However, choose a password that is easy to remember. If you forget it, you may not be able to get at your own data, and if you write it down, it may be discovered and used by someone else. The best passwords include both numbers and letters, so that unauthorized persons will find them less easy to guess.

Backups

Files can be lost or destroyed accidentally. The hard disk may develop problems, or the whole office may be destroyed by fire. You can protect yourself against these nightmare scenarios by keeping backup copies of all your data files, on diskette or another removable medium, and storing it safely at home or at another location. That way, even in the worst situation, you can be up and running very quickly after a disaster.

Backups

> *Copies of software or files on a second storage medium, such as disk or tape, made as a precaution in case the first files are destroyed, lost or corrupted.*

Save frequently

You should also save your work at regular intervals while you are working. Remember that the computer works on your data in working storage (RAM), which is volatile. If there is a power cut, or if someone accidentally unplugs your PC, everything you have done since you last saved will be lost. It is a good discipline to save after every paragraph of text, or after you have done any complex operation.

Viruses

Computer viruses are attempts at sabotage. They are clever but poisonous programs written by malicious software developers and amateur hackers. They attack the integrity of your files, and are designed to transfer easily and stealthily from one computer to another. Their effects vary from minor irritation (where a message is displayed on your screen, but no files are damaged), through inconvenience (where one or more files are affected), to total disaster (where the entire hard disk is rendered unusable).

Viruses are spread through e-mail attachments and the exchange of infected diskettes. So, never open an e-mail attachment if you are unsure of its origin, and always use virus-scanning software to check any diskette that comes into your possession or organization from outside.

Computer Virus

A program that is loaded onto a computer without the user's knowledge and that damages software or data files in some way. Most viruses have the ability to replicate themselves.

Prevention is better than cure: make sure that you install reputable anti-virus software on your computer that will automatically scan your disks (hard drive and diskette), and detect and remove any viruses found. Anti-virus software must be kept up to date – new viruses are being concocted all the time, and the software used to detect them needs to be the very latest.

Data copyright

Remember that computer data carries the same copyright rights and responsibilities as printed works or musical compositions: someone created it, and that person owns it. If you download information from the internet, you may not have the right to include it in your own publications without the consent of the author or creator.

Data protection

We all appear in numerous databases: banks, insurance companies, educational institutions, employers, and governments all hold files full of personal information. Our date of birth, address and marital status, our incomes, credit and educational records, our health, criminal, and bill-paying histories are all known by various institutions. This information is sometimes general, sometimes special. It may be sensitive and, in the wrong hands, damaging or dangerous.

Marketing departments are willing to pay large sums of money for name and address databases of specific categories of people. This enables them to target products and services at precise sectors of the population.

It follows that the collection, maintenance, and protection of information is a responsibility that demands great respect. Wrong or misleading information could lead to a person being refused a mortgage, a job, an overseas work visa, or medical insurance. It could ruin their life. Holding personal information thus demands sensitivity and respect. This is reflected in the *data protection laws*.

Data Protection

The concept that information relating to indiviuals
('personal data'), collected and used by organizations, is
subject to certain regulations.

The European Data Protection Directive

All EU countries either have already adopted laws to give
effect to this EU Directive or will shortly do so.

The Directive requires that all computer-based data be:

- Processed fairly and lawfully

- Collected for specified and explicit purposes

- Adequate, relevant and not excessive

- Accurate and up to date where necessary

- Maintained in a form that means that the data subject
  (that is, the person about whom the data is gathered)
  cannot be identified once their identification is no
  longer necessary.

It is quite common for data to be gathered about internet
users – this enables online businesses to target their
marketing more effectively. Such information is also subject
to the rules on data protection. The EU Directive sets out the
information that must be provided to web users when such
details are collected, including the identity of the collecting
body, the purposes for which the data is intended, the likely
recipients of the data, and the right to access the information
and correct it if it is inaccurate. Each EU Member State must
ensure that controllers of information respect the above rules.

Hacking has worrying implications for data protection. Controllers are required to implement adequate security measures to protect data against accidental or malicious disclosure or access, in particular where the information is being transferred over a network, as in the case of the internet.

One difficulty with the internet is that it is transnational. Data can be transferred from an EU website to a US one at the click of a button. However, the EU Directive prohibits the transfer of information to countries outside the EU unless they have similar protections in place.

Self test 4: Software

1 Is a word processor system software or application software?

2 Is Windows system software or application software?

3 What is the difference between freeware and shareware?

4 Which of the following statements is/are true?

    a ❑ A folder is another name for a diskette.

    b ❑ A file can contain any number of folders.

    c ❑ Records have been made obsolete by CDs.

    d ❑ Files contain records.

5 What is a computer virus?

6 Mention some of the ways to protect your data against loss or corruption.

7 You edit the newsletter for your local community. Are you entitled to sell the mailing list to a marketing company? Why/why not?

Chapter summary: so now you know

A computer is hardware, but it *runs* software. Software determines how the computer behaves – the particular problems it solves at any given time.

System software is inward looking – it is software that controls the computer itself.

Application software is software that addresses a 'real-world' problem – it does something that you or I want done.

Software is developed by *systems analysts* and *programmers* in a process that involves detailed research, analysis, program development, and testing. Testing is almost never comprehensive, so that errors and problems sometimes occur (called bugs).

Licensed software must be purchased and used only under specified conditions.

Shareware is typically available without charge, but a small payment must be made if it is used regularly. Registered users typically receive service assistance and updates.

Freeware is software that, although copyrighted, is given away without charge by its author.

Software belongs to the authors, and, in general, copying it is illegal.

Data is often the most valuable part of a computer system, because it is the least easily replaced. For that reason, you should protect your data against loss or damage by using passwords and anti-virus software. You should also save your work frequently and make *backups* at regular intervals.

You should be especially careful with personal information. The *European Data Protection Directive* imposes specific responsibilities on anyone who maintains databases of personal information.

CHAPTER 5

Networks and the internet

In this chapter

Networking of computers, as you will discover in this chapter, opens up productive and exciting opportunities for sharing resources and information.

As you will also learn, the world's largest network is the internet, which connects millions of computers. Unlike smaller private networks, which are centrally controlled, the internet is decentralized by design.

New skills

At the end of this chapter you should be able to:

- Describe the advantages of computer networking
- Describe the use of the telephone network in computing
- Describe the uses of e-mail, the internet, and the world wide web
- Describe how e-commerce is changing business practices

New words

At the end of this chapter you should be able to explain the following terms:

- Network
- LAN
- WAN
- PSTN
- ISDN
- E-mail
- Internet
- World wide web
- Browser
- Search engine
- e-Commerce

Networks

Computers can function quite happily on their own (*stand-alone computing*), but increasingly they are being connected together into networks.

The advantages of networking

When your computer is connected to other computers – whether they are in the same building or on the other side of the world – it is part of a computer network. You can still use it to do your own work as usual, but several new possibilities open up:

- **Sharing hardware**: In a stand-alone world, people can print only if a printer is attached directly to their computer. By connecting one or more printers to a computer network, everyone whose computer is also attached to the same network can print their documents. Printer sharing means that everyone can print (although not at the same time) without everyone having an individual printer. The same is true of other hardware resources, such as modems, scanners, and plotters.

- **File sharing**: On a stand-alone computer, you can work with all the files stored on your computer's hard disk. On a network-connected computer, you may be able to work with files stored on other people's computers too.

Rather than have network users rummaging through each other's hard disks, information that is needed by everyone in a particular department (in accounts, for example, or in a warehouse) is usually stored on a single, powerful, permanently switched-on computer called a *file server*.

- **e-Mail**: Meetings, telephone conversations, letters and memos – typically, these are the ways in which people in an organization communicate with one another. Computer networks make possible another form of communication called electronic mail, or e-mail for short. This is the exchange of (usually plain-text) messages between users of computers that are connected to a common network.

- **Data exchange**: Users connected to a computer network can exchange files: one person can write an article for the newsletter, another can edit it, a third can lay it out, while a fourth can contribute a drawing or a scanned photograph. This kind of co-operative work over a network is known as *workgroup computing*, or *groupwork*.

Computer network

Two or more computers that are connected together by some means to provide their users with such services as printer sharing, file sharing, and electronic mail.

LANs and WANs

Networks come in two sizes: big and small. A Local Area Network, or LAN, is the kind that connects the computers in a single office, building, or group of adjoining buildings.

Local Area Network (LAN)

A network that connects computers located within a small area.

Large corporations operate computer networks that connect offices at locations within the same or different countries. Such Wide Area Networks, or WANs, can enable, for example:

- The Frankfurt office to exchange e-mails with the Sydney office

- The Tokyo office to read files that are stored on a computer in the New Orleans office

- The Cape Town office to print a report on a printer that is located in the Bombay office

Wide Area Network (WAN)

A network that connects computers over a wide area, typically across international boundaries.

In reality, most networks are bigger than LANs but smaller than WANs. But, for some reason, no one has thought up a name for them.

Computer networks can be open to everyone or restricted to the chosen few. An example of a *private access* network is one operated by a company or government agency for its own personnel only. An example of a *public access* network is the internet.

Making the connection

How do the computers in a network actually connect with one another? Well, in a LAN it's relatively simple: the computers (and printers) are connected together with a special cable. However, in a WAN, that isn't an option. It would be quite impractical to run cables from one side of the country to another, or from one continent to the next.

The telephone network

The solution is that WANs use cables already in place – the cables of the national and international telephone system (the PSTN, or Public Switched Telephone Network). They also use all the other technology of the telephone network – satellites, microwaves, optic fibres, and so on. This has advantages, and one major disadvantage too:

- **Advantages**: It's already in place (so there is no need to run WAN cables across rivers and over mountains), and its connection points are never far away (the phone system reaches into every workplace and virtually every home).

- **Disadvantage**: Computer signals (the ones that travel around inside a computer) are a different 'shape' from the signals accepted by the phone system (ones resulting from the sound of the human voice). Computer signals are 'digital'; voice signals are 'analogue'.

We therefore have a problem: a *signal shape* problem. To connect a computer to a phone line, we need a device than can do two jobs. Which job it does at any particular time depends on the direction of the information transfer:

- **Outgoing information**: When your computer sends data (such as an e-mail) down the phone line, the device must 'shape' the signal – convert it from computer-shape to phone-shape (digital to analog).

- **Incoming information**: When you receive data (such as a file from a distant computer), the device must 'deshape' the signal – reconvert it back from phone-shape to its original computer-shape (analog to digital).

Another, rather poetic, word for the act of shaping anything in this way is *modulation*. A device that shapes (*mod*ulates) and deshapes (*dem*odulates) a signal is called – guess what? – a modem.

Modem

A device that enables computers to communicate over the telephone system. At the sending computer, the modem converts the outgoing data to the format acceptable to the phone system. At the receiving computer, another modem reconverts the data back to its original computer format.

Most modern computers have built-in modems. To connect such a computer to the telephone system, you plug the phone line into the socket at the back of the computer. If your modem is a separate unit, you plug the telephone line into the modem and use another cable to connect the modem to the serial port on the computer. The modem may be battery-powered or may need to be plugged into the mains.

Modems are rated according to the speed at which they can transmit and receive data. The *baud rate* is the number of times the signal changes in one second. However, each change in the signal can carry more than one bit of data, so the measure more commonly used nowadays is *bits per second* or *bps*. The top speed of current modems is around 56 kbps (kilobits per second, or thousands of bits per second).

ISDN

An alternative to using modems and the normal telephone network (PSTN) is to use ISDN, or Integrated Services Digital Network. As its name suggests, this network is designed to carry digital signals. In the past it has been used mainly by businesses that need frequent high-volume communication with other offices, and has been relatively expensive for low-volume users. This is beginning to change – the cost of ISDN is now within the reach of small businesses and home users.

ISDN gives access to two 64 kbps channels; these can be used separately or combined to exchange data at 128 kbps.

e-Mail

Networks enable users to exchange personal messages with one another: this is the idea behind *e-mail*.

To send someone an e-mail message, you need to have a computer connected to a network, and the recipient has to have a computer connected (directly or indirectly) to the same network. You also need e-mail software, and the unique 'address' of the recipient. That's the minimum.

In practice, this means that both of you have:

- A PC

- A modem

- A telephone line

- A subscription to an Internet Service Provider (ISP)

The ISP maintains a continuous connection to the internet, and stores on its computer all e-mail that is sent, from anywhere in the world, to your *mailbox*, until you collect it after submitting a password to prove your entitlement to it.

This system means that you can send a message to your friend even when their computer is turned off: it is stored for them, by their ISP, until they collect it.

Thus, you can carry on an electronic conversation over a period of time, during which neither you nor your friend are ever talking at the same time. This is particularly useful if you live in different time zones.

e-Mail

The exchange of (usually plain-text) messages between users of computers that are connected to a common network.

e-Mail has largely taken over from two earlier technologies that used the telephone network to send and receive written messages:

- **Fax** can be thought of as remote photocopying. The sender used a fax machine to scan a letter, drawing, map, or whatever. The fax machine encoded it so that it could be sent down the telephone line. The

recipient's fax machine decoded the message and
provided a printout.

- **Telex** was a much more primitive technology, which
  acted like a remote typewriter. It accepted only text
  typed on a special telex machine (no pictures). At the
  receiving end, the telex machine responded by typing
  out the same letters and numbers.

The internet

The *internet* – everyone's talking about it. It may even be one
of the main reasons you decided to learn about computers.

The internet
*The internet is a worldwide network of interconnected
networks.*

If you connect to the internet, you can:

- Send e-mail to other users

- Access information stored on computers all around
  the world

Millions of users have access to the internet; hundreds of
thousands of computers are permanently connected to it –
computers owned by governments, universities, companies,
retailers, voluntary organizations, and private individuals. Any
user, anywhere, can send a message to any other user, and can
access files on the other computers. This rich resource can be

used for research, news, entertainment, education, information, sports, current affairs, shopping, and art.

The internet has become by far the most popular network for carrying e-mail, for a number of reasons:

- The network is already in place: there is no need to create a new physical network connecting all the people you want to communicate with.

- It has a huge population of already-connected users: the chances are high that the person you want to communicate with has an internet connection.

- It is designed so that there is no single point of failure – if one computer on the network breaks down, or one phone line fails, the message is routed a different way to avoid the problem.

- It uses common standards: messages sent from one computer system in one country can be received and interpreted correctly by a different computer system in a different country.

World wide web

The term *world wide web* is used to describe documents made available over the internet which are in a particular graphic format. The documents can be linked together, irrespective of where they are physically located, and users can follow the links from document to document. This enables you to pursue a research topic from the general to the specific, from detail to 'big picture', from graphic to text, from text to sound. These links are called hyperlinks, and documents constructed with hyperlinks are called *hypertext*, or *hypermedia* if sound, graphics, or video are involved.

The software used to display world wide web documents (or *web pages*) is called a *browser*. The two most frequently used browsers are Microsoft Internet Explorer and Netscape Navigator.

World wide web

The range of documents published on the internet in a format that enables them to be displayed using a browser.

Browser

A program that enables you to display web pages and follow links from one web page to another.

However, with hundreds of thousands of computers connected to the internet, each with thousands of pages of information available to you, how do you find anything of value?

You use a *search engine* – a program that trawls the internet looking for documents that contain information of interest to you: the share price of a company, flight times from Rome to Athens, comparisons of different brands of vacuum cleaner, the correct spelling of a word in German, the prognosis for a medical condition, tonight's TV listing ... it's all there – somewhere.

Search Engine

A program that searches the world wide web for documents that satisfy your criteria.

Another term used to describe the internet and the world wide web is the *information superhighway*.

e-Commerce

Businesses around the world are beginning to use the internet as a way of developing their markets. They use it to advertise their goods, to take orders, and, in many cases, to deliver their products and services. Obviously only certain kinds of goods can be delivered online, but this includes some that have traditionally been sold in shops, such as software, music, concert tickets, and books. Businesses are also using the internet to find the cheapest or most efficient source of supply of raw materials, to track orders and deliveries, and to communicate with customers.

This move of business to the internet is known as *e-commerce* (or electronic commerce).

The internet can change the way you shop. You can compare prices from different suppliers, buy direct from the manufacturer, or from a supplier anywhere in the world, and communicate with other buyers to get their views on quality and suitability.

When you are making a trip, you can plan your itinerary, find the cheapest flights, look at alternative hotels and compare their facilities and prices, check out special offers, look at maps, and check event listings. You can hire cars, book flights, hotel or guest-house accommodation, concerts, sporting events, even meals in your favourite restaurant.

e-Commerce

Business conducted over a network or the internet. The products and services offered may or may not be available in digital form.

Self test 5: Networks

1 Name two reasons you might connect your computer in a network.

2 The L in LAN stands for:

  a ❏ Leading

  b ❏ Local

  c ❏ Long

  d ❏ Linked

3 The A in WAN stands for:

  a ❏ Access

  b ❏ Attached

  c ❏ Area

  d ❏ Aerial

4 Comment on each of the following statements, indicating whether each is true or false.

  a ❏ Computer networks will shortly make the telephone system obsolete.

  b ❏ Modems are used to increase the speed at which computers can communicate.

  c ❏ The telephone system is ideally suited for communication between computers.

  d ❏ e-Mail is another name for the internet.

5 What is the internet? State two of the most common uses of the internet.

6   What is the world wide web? What kind of software do you need to use it?

7   What is a search engine?

8   Give some examples of e-commerce.

9   What kinds of goods and services are most easily traded over the internet?

10 For one of the following businesses, say how its business could be changed by e-commerce: travel agent, record company, supermarket, restaurant, hairdresser.

Chapter summary: so now you know

Computer *networking* enables users to share resources such as hardware and data, and to exchange messages. This kind of co-operative work over a network is known as *workgroup computing*, or *groupwork*. Networks may cover a small area (local area networks or *LANs*) or a larger region (wide area networks or *WANs*).

WANs typically use the telephone system (the PSTN) to establish connections between distant computer users. This requires the use of a *modem*. Telephone companies increasingly offer *ISDN* services for high-speed computer communications.

To use *e-mail*, the sender and the receiver must each have a PC, a modem, access to a telephone line, and a subscription to an internet service provider (or other e-mail carrier).

The *internet* is a worldwide network of interconnected networks. It is by far the most common medium for e-mail, and also provides the infrastructure for the *world wide web*. The world wide web is a vast array of documents that are available over the internet in a particular format – a format that enables them to be displayed with a browser. The *browser* enables you to display the document of your choice, and to follow hyperlinks from one document to another. A *search engine* is a program that trawls the internet looking for documents that contain information of interest.

The internet is enabling many businesses to reach new markets and offer new services to customers around the world. This is known as *e-commerce*.

CHAPTER 6

What computers are used for

In this chapter

In this chapter we take a look at some of the ways in which computers are used, and the effects they have on our lives. This isn't comprehensive – it can't be, as new uses are being found every day. However, by the end of the chapter, you should appreciate that the range of applications is very wide indeed.

New skills

At the end of this chapter you should be able to:
- Discuss the widespread use of computers in modern society
- Offer examples of computer application in business, industry, schools, health care, and the home
- Discuss appropriate and inappropriate uses of computers
- Discuss the information society

Business and administration

Most offices today depend on computers. Computers are used to keep accounts, to send invoices, to maintain records of customers and suppliers, to hold details of stock, to calculate payroll, to write and edit letters, memos and reports, to design sales presentations, to communicate with other companies, to collect market intelligence, to collaborate with others in research activities.

Computers are also used in more complex business processes such as resource planning, scheduling, route planning, customer relationship management, sales analysis, and simulation.

Computers are particularly useful where there are large volumes of data to be maintained, analysed, stored and filtered, or where complex or repetitive calculations have to be performed.

Industry

In the manufacturing industry, the range of applications includes all of the administrative functions mentioned above, and a whole lot more besides. Computers are used to schedule production, to monitor raw material usage and finished product quality, to control machine tools, to design new products, to minimize waste, and to determine optimum stock levels.

In most automated plants, computers are used to collect orders from customers, to issue instructions to build the required products to the customer's specifications, to order the parts and materials automatically from the relevant subsuppliers (having first checked that they can deliver on time), and to schedule the plant and personnel necessary for satisfying the customer's order.

Retailing

In supermarkets, and increasingly in smaller shops, computers are used at the checkout to scan the bar codes on your purchases, and to calculate your bill. In many stores the information on your purchases is passed immediately to the warehouse, and orders for replacement stock are generated automatically when stock falls below a given point. Instructions can also be generated for the personnel responsible for stacking the shelves, so that the products are always available. This technology enables the supermarket to keep its stock to the minimum necessary to satisfy its customers, instead of having money tied up unnecessarily in stock and storage space.

Computers can also be used to control moving-message advertising panels. These displays are made up of hundreds of *light-emitting diodes* (LEDs) that are turned on and off rapidly to create text and pictures.

Home

In the home, computers have found a wide variety of uses – for playing games (most often), keeping household accounts, getting information over the internet (to research ancient history for a homework project or for checking the scores in the Italian football league), and for sending e-mail to friends and relatives abroad. The list grows every day, and imagination is the only limit.

Many people have established professional design studios and desktop publishing businesses at home using PCs. Others have managed to use their PCs to offer desktop video or sound editing comparable to that offered by expensive and sophisticated dedicated equipment. Book-keepers and accountants, journalists and writers, and database designers are also able to work from home nowadays, thanks to the PC and connectivity.

Schools

When you hear about young people using computers in schools, you may think they are doing something very technical, like programming, or electronics. They seldom are.

The main uses for computers in schools are in the traditional subject areas. There is a lot of educational software available that presents school subjects in a structured and entertaining way. Some students respond better to information presented in this way, and computers also enable each student to progress at his or her own pace – the computer will repeat lessons as often as necessary, without losing patience!

In addition, the computer opens up the school to the outside world. Students can retrieve information from libraries, universities, government agencies, voluntary bodies, news organizations, and other

sources. They can communicate with students in other countries, and co-operate with them on research projects. They can take lessons from world experts without leaving their classroom.

In some science subjects, computers can be used to simulate experiments that are either dangerous or expensive. This enables the students to learn without exposing themselves to the dangers, or without incurring the costs of the materials of equipment involved in the experiment.

Students can also use the computer to write reports, produce school newsletters, and design posters.

Health care

The administration of hospitals depends more and more on computers. In fact, many of the applications are similar to manufacturing: scheduling expensive and scarce equipment, drawing up rosters, making appointments for patients, etc. In addition, computers are used for monitoring patients' conditions and alerting staff when abnormalities arise. Computers also allow doctors to keep comprehensive patient records, and to conduct research into the effectiveness of different treatments.

Research is also heavily dependent on computing power: most modern drugs are designed with the aid of computers and manufactured under computer control. The human genome project, which promises major breakthroughs in the treatment of genetic disorders, would be impossible without powerful computers.

Computers and communications technology are also being used to deliver health services to remote regions: the patient can connect to a major centre (or a centre of specialist expertise) for diagnosis and, in some cases, for treatment. This development is expected to yield significant cost-savings and better treatment for patients in the coming years.

Government and public administration

Government agencies use computers for a wide range of purposes, in the same way as businesses – for accounting, stock control, project management, budgeting, forecasting, and so on. The main difference is one of scale: in general, governments need to maintain very large bodies of information – registers of births, marriages and deaths; tax and social welfare records; census of population data; voting registers, for example. It would be almost impossible, today, to maintain these records in a usable condition without computers.

Everyday life

You would recognize the computers used in the applications outlined so far. However, computer technology is also used in less visible ways. Computers control the cycles in your washing machine, the timer in your video recorder, the sequences of the traffic lights, the delivery of money through an automatic teller machine, and the supply of fuel to your car engine. Almost anywhere you see something happening 'automatically', there is a computer at its heart, monitoring the outside world and responding to it.

Speech synthesizers are programs that produce computer-generated speech in imitation of the human voice. They are increasingly used in telephone applications such as directory enquiries, voicemail systems, telephone banking, and travel information systems. They are also used to enable blind or partially sighted people to use computers: the speech synthesizer 'reads' aloud any text that appears on the screen.

Information technology and society

Some people find this proliferation of computers somewhat disturbing. Is there no aspect of our lives that is untouched by computers? Are computers replacing people, creating unemployment? Are all uses of computers good, or are computers being used to manipulate and control us? Are all computer-assisted services and all computer-manufactured goods better than their predecessors?

These questions don't have clear-cut answers.

From the discussion in this chapter, you probably agree that the society we live in uses computers a lot, and that many of the goods we consume and many of the services we use would not be available without computers. Like it or not, we are living in the Computer Age, or the Information Age, or the Digital Age (take your pick), and our society can justifiably be called an *information society*. In essence this means that value in the society comes from information.

In the Age of Agriculture, most of the work, and most of the value, related to food production. In the Industrial Age, it was manufacturing that defined the society. The availability of food was almost taken for granted; proportionately less time and effort went into ensuring the food supply to the individual. Value, wealth and incomes depended more on manufactured goods.

In recent years, the balance has shifted again, this time towards service occupations – office-based occupations, in which information, knowledge, and intelligence play the key role. The emphasis has been transferred from brawn to brain. And in this new economy, computers play a critical, central role.

It is worth asking, however, whether all uses of computers are good. We can see the benefit of using computers, for example, to process bank transactions. Would we be equally happy to let computers decide loan approvals? Routine administration of, say, parking fines could usefully be delegated to computers, but what about putting computer systems in the role of judges in court? In medicine and health care, there are many obvious useful applications, and there are other applications that make many people uncomfortable.

In the world of art, there are also difficulties: does computer-generated 'art' deserve the name? Can a computer write poetry, make paintings, compose music? And should we judge these 'creations' by the same criteria that we judge work made by humans?

As we said, these questions do not have clear-cut answers. But it is worth thinking about them, because they are becoming increasingly relevant to everyday life.

Participation in the Information Society

Computers and related technologies affect our lives from the time the electronic alarm clock wakes us up to the time we use the remote control to turn off the television at night. We can respond as passive consumers of entertainment and advertising, or by becoming active participants in this society.

Participation means exercising choice: choice about what information we get, when we get it, in what form we get it, and how we use it. It means analyzing the information for relevance, salience, and accuracy. It means deciding what to keep, and what to discard. It means deciding what to produce: what to publish, to whom you publish it, in what form, and at what time.

The idea of the ECDL – and the idea of this book – is to enable you to use some of the tools necessary for this kind of active participation in the information society.

However, you already have the most important tools, and you know how to use them: your natural intelligence, your critical faculties, the ability to judge whether or not something makes sense. No amount of technology can replace these, and you should never be so blinded by technological wizardry that you doubt these innate talents.

Self test 6: Computers in society

1   Which of the following statements do you agree with, and why?

   a   ❑   Computers are faster than humans at mathematical calculations.

b ❑ Humans have more reliable long-term memory than computers.

c ❑ Computers can be programmed to write poetry.

d ❑ Computers can diagnose and treat medical conditions better than doctors.

2 Name some of the ways in which your local supermarket uses computers. Say how each of these affects the management, the staff, and the customers.

3 What does the term *information society* mean?

4 Who benefits from the transition to an information society? What problems might arise?

5 'The information society will involve gross invasions of personal privacy.' Discuss.

Chapter summary: so now you know

Computers are used in business, in industry, in retailing, in the home, in schools and colleges, in health care, in public administration, and in almost every aspect of everyday life.

It is worthwhile pausing every so often to consider whether every possible application of computers is necessarily a good one. Some things are best left to human beings, exercising human judgement, and bringing human values to bear.

And it is also worth considering what this proliferation of computers into every aspect of modern life means for society. There is a danger that society will be divided into those who have access to computers and know how to use

them (the 'information rich'), and those that have no access
to computers or don't know how to use them (the
'information poor').

The ECDL will equip you with the skills to participate in
the information society, but you will increasingly need to
exercise your critical faculties: remember that all the
information available on the internet, for example, was
created and input by someone, somewhere. And that
'someone' could be biased, misguided, prejudiced, or just
plain wrong.

CHAPTER 7

Looking after number one: health and safety

In this chapter

This chapter deals with something even more valuable than hardware, software, or data. Something irreplaceable – you.

Just as we have accustomed ourselves to using safety belts and child-proof locks in cars, we need to adopt safe computing practices. Problems can arise in a number of areas, but sensible precautions can help you avoid them.

In general, computers are clean, quiet, and safe to use. You should be aware, however, of a number of potential dangers, and how to avoid them.

New skills

At the end of this chapter you should be able to:
- Describe some of the hazards associated with using a computer
- Describe sensible computing practices

New words

At the end of this chapter you should be able to explain the following term:
- Repetitive strain injury

Repetitive strain injury

I f you do any physical activity for a long time without a break, you risk straining or injuring yourself. Using a keyboard or mouse for a prolonged period can lead to the computer user's equivalent of tennis elbow. It can affect the fingers, hands, wrists, elbows, or even the back. The best way to avoid this problem is to take a break every fifteen or twenty minutes to allow your muscles to rest and recuperate.

Repetitive strain injury
> *Damage to tendons, nerves, muscles and other soft body tissues resulting from repeated physical movements.*

You should also make sure your desk and chair are at a suitable height, and that your keyboard is at a comfortable angle (see below).

Eyesight

Extended periods of staring at a PC screen can lead to fatigue and ultimately to eye-strain. Avoid locking your eyes into a fixed screen stare. Look away frequently and focus your eyes on objects on the other side of the room, or out the window. Make sure that your work area is adequately lit and ventilated.

Posture

Simple ergonomics are often so obvious that they are overlooked. You should arrange the hardware elements of your PC in such a way as to provide the easiest and most physically comfortable access. Your desk should support your screen at the correct eye level. Your chair should be comfortable, adjustable, and provide adequate lumbar support.

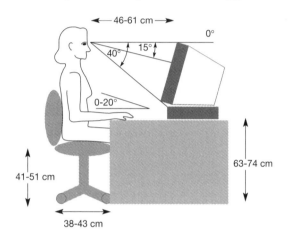

Accidents

Your computer system includes a number of different physical devices. They are all connected together by cables. The system unit is plugged into the mains electricity socket. On some models the screen takes its electricity supply from the system unit; in others it plugs directly into the mains. The speakers are usually plugged into the mains. The modem is connected to the telephone socket.

That's a lot of cables and wires. Make sure that the cables connecting the components are kept tidy, secure, and out of the way, so that there is no danger of tripping over them. Also make sure that the mains electricity sockets you use are capable of handling the load safely: don't plug all the appliances into a single adaptor or you risk overloading the circuit.

Self test 7: Using your computer safely

1 Which of the following is/are true?

    a ❑ It is best to get all your data entry done in the morning, while you are fresh.

    b ❑ You should sit as close to the screen as possible, so that you don't strain your eyes.

    c ❑ If you sit too close to the screen, you can catch a computer virus.

    d ❑ The best way to avoid repetitive strain injury (RSI) is to continue working after you feel pain. That way, your arm muscles develop faster.

2 If you are using a computer for a long time, the best kind of chair is:

    a ❑ An office chair that can be adjusted for height

    b ❑ A dining chair with arm supports

    c ❑ A comfortable sofa

3 True or false: In winter, it is a good idea to cover the system unit with a blanket, so that it doesn't get cold.

4 State some of the dangers associated with using a computer, and how to minimize them.

Chapter summary: so now you know

While using a computer is generally safe, there are a number of hazards, and all of them are avoidable. Most of them – in particular *repetitive strain injury* and eye strain – arise only if you use the computer for long periods without a break. Others arise from bad posture or inappropriate positioning of equipment. Cabling also presents a potential source of accidents: you should make sure that cables are tidy and out of the way.

Answers to self tests

Self test 1: History of computing

1   c
2   a: Controlling fuel/air mix, distributing power or braking to wheels, security
     b: Timing, eliminating distortion
     c: Checking account balances, verifying personal identification
     d: Not typical, but possibly providing speedometer and odometer, or pulse monitor
3   False
4   False

Self test 2: A computer is ...?

1   c and d
2   b and d
3   b
4   a
5   c and d
6   b

Self test 3: Hardware

1   a
2   a
3   A scanner is used to capture images for use in a computer application.
4   A modem is used to connect a computer to the telephone network.
5   b
6   b
7   a
8   b: A megabyte is a million bytes.
    c: 1,000,000,000 bytes is equal to a GB.
9   a, c, d, and e
10 Mouse, joystick, trackball, light pen, games controller, touch screen.
11 Laser and inkjet.
12 Zip disk.

Self test 4.1: Software

1   Application software.
2   Systems software.
3   No payment is required for freeware.
4   d
5   Malicious programs designed to disrupt the normal operation of a computer or corrupt its files.
6   Save frequently; use password protection; take regular backups; use up-to-date anti-virus software.
7   No. The list was collected for one purpose and may not be used for another without the consent of everyone on the list.

Self test 4.2: Networks

1   Exchange e-mail; exchange or share files; share hardware resources.

2   b

3   c

4 a: False – computers are a major part of modern telephone systems, and major users of them.

  b: False – modems are necessary for computers to communicate over the telephone network.

  c: False – not ideal – while the telephone system has the advantage of being in place, it was designed for voice communication.

  d: False– e-mail is one of the major uses for the internet.

5   A worldwide network of interconnected networks.

6   A vast range of documents available on the internet in a format that enables them to be displayed with browser software.

7   A program that searches the world wide web for documents that match your criteria.

8   Sales of books or CDs over the internet; electronic banking; comparing the price of goods using online catalogues; booking concert tickets on the internet.

9   Non-perishable goods; goods with high value-to-weight ratio; information services; digital content.

10   Travel agent: Accept bookings by e-mail or via a web site; reserve airline tickets, hotel rooms, hire cars, etc., via internet; provide better customer services to a wider client base via website.

     Record company: Use web site to promote artists and releases; provide samples on website; deliver albums or individual tracks as MP3 files; run competitions and promotions.

Supermarket: Provide online ordering facility backed up by home delivery service; attract loyal customers with special promotions, etc.; link sales to supplier orders to ensure just-in-time replenishment of stock.

Restaurant: Promote via website showing menu, special offers, etc.; take reservations online – including letting customer choose his or her own table; keep in touch with customers via e-mail.

Hairdresser: Promote new styles, products, special offers, etc., on a website; allow customers to make appointments with their preferred stylist; generate customer loyalty by keeping in touch by e-mail.

Self test 5: Computers in society

(Note: Answers to this test should not be treated as absolute. Discuss them with your friends and fellow students. Disagree. Debate.)

1. a: Agree, under most circumstances
   b: Disagree, again under most circumstances – but when a computer fails, it fails completely
   c: Disagree – it may look like poetry, it may sound like poetry ... but is it poetry?
   d: Disagree – as long as the condition is complex, human judgement is required.
2. Checkout scanning: Makes stock control easier; makes life very tedious for staff; customers are checked out quicker, with fewer errors.

Stock Control: Ensures that products are always available, without keeping excess stock; helps staff to identify products that are running low and need to be restocked; customers should benefit from product availability and lower prices.

Office Administration: Rostering staff, payroll, accounting; staff benefit from smooth running organisation; customers don't really see the benefit, but indirectly benefit from the smoother operation.

3   The term is used to describe a society in which most of the value relates to information products and services.

4   Those who benefit are those who are involved with the production of information goods or services, or who can afford to consume them. Problems can arise if the benefits are concentrated in the hands of relatively few people, or if significant segments of society are excluded by not having access to or the ability to use the information goods or services.

5   Discuss

Self test 6: Using your computer safely

1   None is true

2   a

3   False

4   Repetitive strain injury (take regular breaks; choose suitable furniture); eye strain (rest your eyes by looking away from the screen frequently); accidents (make sure cables are secure and tidy; don't overload electricity sockets).